Disclosure

All of the information provided in this guide has been verified and is accurate as of 11/14/13. For updated info, please contact your respective mystery shopping provider.

Although I've shopped with many of the companies listed here, I am an independent contractor and do not profit from readers clicking on links, signing up, or completing any assignments.

Index/Table of Contents

Introduction

If you're interested in becoming a mystery shopper, this guide will help you get started.

You've probably heard of mystery shoppers making upwards of $10,000 per month. While most assignments are time-consuming and pay around $10, you can still make a nice supplemental income as a mystery shopper, while enjoying your favorite restaurants, retail stores, spas, hotels, and more!

With mystery shopping scams running rampant, the next step is to find a list of legitimate companies you can trust.

I've been a mystery shopper for three years and have shopped for numerous companies, which are listed under **Tried and Tested Companies**. At the end of this guide, you will also find a comprehensive **List of Legitimate Companies**.

All of the companies listed in this guide are members of the **Mystery Shopping Providers Association (MSPA)**. The MSPA sets strict guidelines for membership, minimizing scams.

The MSPA also lists assignments on its website and regularly offers certification courses for shoppers. In my experience, you do not need a certificate to get desirable assignments, but it never hurts to increase your knowledge and skill set.

How it works

1. Register. Register with one or more of the MSPA- member mystery shopping companies. This can be as easy as filling out a profile, to an extensive application process requiring essay questions.

You will be asked to provide your social security number at registration, which is needed for payment processing. Some companies will let you skip this until you've actually completed an assignment.

If you live in Nevada, you will need a worker's card to be a mystery shopper (see pg. 13).

2. Search. Search for assignments in your area, using the respective company's assignment search engine. You can save time by searching the MSPA's assignment database.

Sometimes if coordinators are pressed to get assignments completed, they will email or call shoppers, offering additional incentives. Helping a coordinator will earn you priority over other shoppers when in-demand assignments become available.

Evaluator/Shopper: Mystery shopper

Shop Coordinator/Scheduler: Assigns jobs to mystery shoppers.

---

3. **Apply for assignments.** Some companies allow you to self-assign instantly, while others review applicant profiles and choose shoppers based on score. You will often complete training modules and take a quiz prior to being assigned, to prepare you and determine your suitability for the job.

4. **Prepare.** Once you've been approved for an assignment, you'll receive detailed instructions along with a survey. Read the instructions very carefully. Failing to do so can result in mistakes that jeopardize your payment for the assignment as well as your status as a mystery shopper with that company.

Before beginning your assignment, read through the survey. It's best to visualize your visit and identify possible scenarios when specific questions might get answered. Sometimes coordinators will call to remind you of your upcoming assignment and prepare you for it. Use this opportunity to get answers to any questions you may have.

It's also a good idea to keep your shop coordinator's phone number handy in case you run into problems while on assignment (more on that in "Tips & Advice").

5. Complete your assignment. Some companies will let shoppers chose a shop date and offer flexibility on report submissions, while others have strict deadlines. Make sure you are aware of deadlines before applying for assignments.

If you've read your instructions and know which aspects of the visit you'll be evaluating, the assignment will be much easier.

Behave as a normal shopper would. This means, no writing notes or excessive texting. If you want to text information to yourself (start time, end time, etc.), do this discreetly. Compromising your anonymity will not only invalidate your assignment and jeopardize your pay, but may hinder your ability to get assignments in the future.

6. Report back. Reports can be as simple as a brief survey, to a long and detailed narrative. By now you will have read the instructions and know what is expected of you. If you do need to write a narrative, be as detailed as possible. Your report will be numerically graded (1-10) and determine your eligibility for future assignments.

Many companies will reserve the best assignments for their highest-rated shoppers, so your report is a key factor in determining future job eligibility.

Make sure you meet report deadlines or contact your shop coordinator if you need an extension. Otherwise, you risk partial or no payment.

7. Follow ups. Be prepared to answer follow up questions from editors, especially if your report isn't as thorough as they need it to be. Editors will also contact you regarding any inconsistencies in your report, so make sure your report is honest and accurate. Failure to respond to follow-up inquiries will result in no payment for the assignment, and you will be banned from shopping with the company again.

8. Get Paid. Payment for assignments can vary. Most mystery shopping companies will pay shoppers at the end of the following month. Others, including BestMark, will pay in about 2 weeks. The payment schedule varies by company, as does the method. You will either receive a check or payment through Paypal.

Tips & Advice

1. Remain anonymous. If at any time your anonymity is compromised, you've made a mistake, or forgotten to evaluate a certain aspect of your visit, <u>call your coordinator immediately</u> to get further instructions. Sometimes the assignment can be salvaged, partial payment will be offered, or the evaluation will be rescheduled. It's important to be honest and notify your coordinator of any problems.

2. Beware of scammers. Never respond to any company recruitment email or letters. Scammers will pose as legitimate companies. They will offer high pay and ask for money to cover "training expenses" or a membership fee.

Legitimate mystery shopping companies will never ask you for start-up or membership fees.

3. Wait close to the end of the month to sign up for assignments. This is recommended for two reasons: 1.) As the month comes to an end, evaluation fees go up substantially as coordinators scramble to get assignments completed. I have regularly completed a $7 tobacco evaluation for $25 by waiting until the end of the month. 2.) Most companies pay shoppers at the end of the month following their assignment completion (i.e. If you complete your assignment in November, you'll be paid at the end of December). This minimizes wait time to get paid.

4. Start slow. Mystery shopping assignments can be as quick as answering a brief survey to requiring a detailed narrative (I once wrote 8 pages of narrative for a spa evaluation!). Therefore I don't recommend doing more than 1-2 assignment per day to start. Tobacco compliance shops are the easiest, requiring as little as a 5-question survey with basic information (time/date of assignment, name and description of cashier, were you asked for ID?).

Retail assignments require a bit more time, as you'll have to spend a minimum of 20 minutes in the store, memorize details of your interaction with employees, evaluate various aspects of your visit, and report back with a narrative.

5. Write a good narrative. When writing a narrative, don't skimp on necessary details. Read the instructions and edit your report accordingly. Most companies look for the following details in a report:

1.) Name and description of staff (gender, hair color, eye color, height, approximate age range). Generally, it is not a good idea to include info about race.

2.) Time and date of assignment (time you entered facility, time you were helped, time you left).

3.) Explanation of service points that were evaluated, especially if standards were not met.

4.) Narrative of your visit.

For restaurant evaluations, you will often be asked to record the time you were greeted, seated, served, checked on, etc. Do not provide exact times if you are unsure of them. For example, instead of writing "At 1:25 PM, we walked into the restaurant and at 1:28 PM we were seated," use "We entered the restaurant at 1:25 PM and were seated about three minutes later."

Provide an objective narrative, unless otherwise asked. Do not express any opinions in your report, unless instructed to do so. Simply state the facts of your experience. Do not state how you felt or what you thought (i.e. "The clerk seemed agitated"). Instead use facts ("The clerk spoke in an abrasive tone").

6. Hold on to your receipts. You will be asked to include a copy of your receipt along with your report, in order to get reimbursed. Many companies will also ask that you hold on to your original receipt and any materials collected for the assignment (brochures, cards, etc.) **for up to 6 months**, in case of an audit. You must be able to present these documents upon request.

7. Cancellations/No shows: Call your coordinator to reschedule, or you may get banned for being a no-show.

8. Get a Nevada workers card. These can be obtained from the <u>Nevada Private Investigators Licensing Board</u>. The total cost is roughly $120. However, BestMark reimburses this cost once you complete 3 Nevada assignments for them. Be sure to verify this with BestMark prior to beginning the process, as their policy may change.

- Application + $95 fee (if fingerprints mailed) or $85 if submitted electronically.
- 1 passport size photo ($7.99)
- 2 fingerprint cards or receipt for electronic submission. ($15)
- Proof if ID (i.e. copy of passport, driver's license, birth certificate, etc.)

List of Tried & Tested Companies

1.) Beyond Hello
Assignment types: Retail, coffee shops, restaurants, car dealerships, outlets.

2.) Confero, Inc.
Assignment types: Tobacco compliance, fast food, amusement parks, car rental.

3.) Coyle Hospitality
Assignment types: Rigorous selection process. Evaluators have access to desirable assignments including: High-end restaurants, hotels, spas, cruises, baseball games, apartment evaluations, phone reservations, and more. Pay is quick and travel reimbursement are generous (usually $950 for international travel, $125 for domestic).

4.) Customer Impact
Assignment types: Retail, fast food, home improvement.

5.) Intelli-Shop
Assignment types: Oil change, car dealerships, retail, fast food.

6.) KSS International, Inc.
Assignment types: Tobacco compliance, banks, retail.

7.) Reality Based Group
Assignment types: Parking garage, fast food, oil change.

8.) Service Check

Assignment types: Warehouse, retail, bank, YMCA.

9.) DSG Associates

Assignment types: Banks, credit unions.

10.) BestMark

Assignment types: Electronic stores (Best Buy), restaurants (Applebee's). Vegas hotel/casino assignments pay around $75. If you obtain a Nevada work card and complete 3 assignments, they will reimburse your expenses for obtaining your card. Pays 1-2 weeks after job completion.

11.) Corporate Research International

Assignment types: Lowe's, Kmart, Aeropostale. Low pay at $4-7 each. Also has a survey panel, which pays $1-$50 per survey. Must complete CRI Auditor University courses to qualify for assignments.

12.) ICCDS

Assignment types: Jamba Juice, Coach, Footlocker. Decent pay.

13.) Market Force

Assignment types: Grocery stores, restaurants, check cash scenarios, gas station evaluations, retail, airport shops.

14.) Service Intelligence

Assignment types: Offers lucrative trade school evaluations (paying upwards of $75 each), tobacco compliance ($7-30).

Complete List of Legitimate Companies

Company Name
A Closer Look
A Top Shop!
AboutFace
ACE Mystery Shopping
Advisory Group Associates, LLC
Albatross Global Solutions
Amusement Advantage, Inc.
Ann Michaels & Associates, Ltd.
Archon Development Corp.
Ardent Services, Inc.

Company Name
At Your Service Marketing
Ath Power Consulting Corporation
Automotive Insights, LLC
Baird Consulting
Bare International
BDS Marketing
BestMark
Beyond Hello
Big K Mystery Shopping
BMA Mystery Shopping
Business Evaluation Services

Company Name
CALIBER Mystery Shopping
CIMA Research, LLC
Circle of Service, LLC
Cirrus Marketing Intelligence
ClientSmart
Coast to Coast Scheduling Services
Confero, Inc.
Constance Anderson and Associates
Consumer Impressions
Consumer Service Analysis
Consumer@Site

Company Name
Core Research
Corporate Research International
Corporate Risk Solutions
Coyle Hospitality Group
Creative Image Associates
CRG Mystery Shopping
Cross Financial Group
Customer 1st
Customer Experience Experts
Customer Feedback, LLC
Customer Impact, LLC

Company Name
Customer Perspectives
Customer Service Experts
Customer Service Profiles, LLC
DSG Associates
Dynamic Advantage
Ellis Partners in Mystery Shopping
Feedback Plus
Freeman Group Measurement
Frontline Focus International
GAP Buster
GfK Mystery Shopping

Company Name
GigWalk
Goodwin & Associates
Grass Roots America
Greenhouse Marketing & Communications
GuestCheck
Harland Clarke
Hospitality Now
HS Brands International
ICC/Decision Services
ICU Associates
iMyst

Company Name
Informa Research Services
InnerDrive Strategies
Instant-Replays
Insula Research
Integrity Consultants
IntelliShop
In-Touch Insight Systems
IPSOS Mystery Shopping
J.D. Power and Associates
Jancyn Evaluation Shops
Kinesis-CEM

Company Name
KSS International
LRA Worldwide
Maritz Research
Market Force Information
Marketing Endeavors
Market Wise Consulting Group
MASSolutions
Matrix Hospitality Management
Management Consultant Group
Measure Consumer Perspectives
Melinda Brody and Co.

Company Name
Mercantile Systems
Mintel International Group
Monterey Mystery Shopping
MSP Services, LLC dba Mystery Shopper Pros
mVentix
Mystery Researchers
Mystery Shoppers
Mystique Shopper
National Shopping Service
Nationwide Services Group
New Image Marketing

Company Name
Northwest Loss Prevention Consultant
Opinions
Perception Strategies
Person to Person Quality
Pinnacle Financial
Premier Service
Primo Solutions
ProVantage Corporate Analytics
QSI Specialists
Quality Assessments Mystery Shoppers
Quest for Best/Quest Associates

Company Name
Reality Based Group/GameFilm
Reality Check
Regal Hospitality Group
Remington Evaluations
RetailTrack Mystery Shopping & Consulting
RitterAssociates
Sales Quality Research Group
Second To None
Secret Shopper (Sights on Service, Inc.)
Sentry Marketing Group
Service Evaluation Concepts

Company Name
Service Excellence Group
Service Intelligence
Service Performance Group
Service Scan
Shopmetrics
Shop'n Chek Mexico
Shoppers Critique International
Shoppers' View
Shoppers, Inc
Sinclair Customer Metrics
Six Star Solutions

Company Name
Spot Check Services
Statopex, Inc.
Summit Scheduling and Editing
Surf Merchants
Taylor & Associates
Texas Shoppers Network
The Shadow Agency Inc.-Newmark
TrendSource
Verify International
Winthrop Douglas

www.ingramcontent.com/pod-product-compliance
Lightning Source LLC
Chambersburg PA
CBHW081422170526
45166CB00010B/3438